SANITATION WORKER EXAM PREP BOOK
NEW YORK CITY EDITION

by
www.nyccivilserviceexams.com

REVISED EDITION
January 2015

The information in this guide is for informational purposes only. We are not guaranteeing that you will pass the exam. Information given in this book do not reflect official rules, procedures, laws. The rules, laws, etc. that have been provided are for information purposes only. For up to date and official laws, you should contact appropriate agencies and departments. Similarity of any names of people, places, are coincidental.

All rights reserved including the reproduction in whole or in part in any form or by any means.

©2015 All Rights Reserved
www.nyccivilserviceexams.com

ABOUT THIS BOOK

The Sanitation Worker Exam will not be based on your knowledge of the Sanitation Department. As noted in the Notice of Examination, "the multiple choice test is designed to assess certain abilities determined to be important to the performance of the tasks of a Sanitation Worker. The test may include questions requiring the use of any of the following abilities" :

Written & Reading Comprehension: understanding written sentences and paragraphs. This ability may be used to read and understand departmental messages.

Problem Sensitivity: being able to tell when something is wrong or is likely to go wrong. It includes being able to identify the whole problem as well as elements of the problem. This ability may be used to tell if there is something wrong with the truck, which will lead to a mechanical failure.

Written Expression: using English words or sentences in writing so that others will understand. This ability may be used to complete a form for a specific request such as switching a vacation day.

Information Ordering; following correctly a rule or set of rules or actions in a certain order. The rule or set of rules used must be given. The things or actions to be put in order can include numbers, letters, works, pictures, procedures, sentences, and mathematical or logical operations. This ability may be used to understand the correct order in which a plow must be assembled.

Deductive Reasoning: applying general rules to specific problems and coming up with logical answers. It involves deciding if an answer makes sense. This ability may be used to determine which type of waste to collect, based on specific waste collection rules.

Spatial Orientation: determining where you are in relation to the location of some object of where the object is in relation to you. This ability may be used to determine where to drive in order to get to your supervisor located a few blocks away.

Visualization: imagining how something would look when it is moved around or when its parts are moved or rearranged. It requires the forming of mental images of how patterns or objects would look after certain changes, such as unfolding or rotation. One has to predict how an object, set of objects, or pattern will appear after the changes have been carried out. This ability may be used to assemble a plow based on an illustration.

PSYCHOMETRICS & THE SANITATION WORKER EXAM

Although you will not see it mentioned anywhere, these types of skills are known as some of the fundamentals of PSYCHOMETRICS. Employers everywhere, give these Psychometric tests as part of the application process for a particular job/career. Psychometrics comes from the Greek work psycho (mind), metria (measure). So essentially it is the 'measuring of the mind'. Typical Psychometrics Testing is broken into two parts: the Personality section of the test, and the Aptitude section of the test.

The Personality section of the test is not applicable for this exam, but the other part of Psychometrics section is.

Psychometrics measure:
Spatial Reasoning
Reading Comprehension
Verbal Reasoning
Numerical Reasoning

Although this exam will not measure your knowledge about the inner workings of the Sanitation Department, in developing the questions in this book we tried to relate them to practical on the job experiences and/or typical Sanitation type job duties and issues. We believe that no knowledge is wasted or not necessary....

" - *Knowledge is power.*
      Sir Francis Bacon-

THE RECIPE FOR PASSING

It would be misleading and inaccurate for any exam prep book to promise that if you buy and study their book you will be guaranteed to pass the exam.

Our goal with this book is to give you examples of the types of questions you can expect and for you to identify which areas you could use some improvement in.

So "Why you ask, should I identify what I need improvement with? I bought this book to study and help me pass, not tell me what problems I have." With any problem, if you can clearly identify your problem or your weakness only then you can begin working on it.

- Read and study this book
- Identify what you areas you need improvement with
- Practice even more with the Additional Bonus Study Resources and methods we provide you with

Now after you've done these 3 steps, we will not guarantee you will pass, but we believe you will score a lot higher on the exam than if you didn't follow our RECIPE FOR PASSING.

Remember that the higher you score on the exam, the better your chances for getting selected for the job. Even 1 point can make a difference.

www.nyccivilserviceexams.com

Contents

Introduction..2-5

Chapter 1: Written & Reading Comprehension............8

Chapter 2: Problem Sensitivity...........................16

Chapter 3: Written Expression............................21

Chapter 4: Information Ordering.........................29

Chapter 5: Deductive Reasoning..........................33

Chapter 6: Spatial Orientation...........................41

Chapter 7: Mathematics....................................45

Chapter 8: Visualization...................................52

Chapter 9: Laws & Regulations...........................59

Chapter 10: Glossary - Helpful Terms to Know................65

Bonus Study Resources Section............................71

GOOD LUCK! and more COMING SOON.....................73

SANITATION WORKER EXAM PREP BOOK

Chapter 1: Written & Reading Comprehension

Questions 1 through 5 are to be answered SOLELY on the basis of the information given in the following passage.

On October 29th, 2012 Hurricane Sandy made her presence known in New York City, and she made certain to leave a lasting impression. The start of the rainfall opened a Pandora's Box, and it took more than a good bit of time to close it shut again. Between the resulting injuries and fatalities, the abundant amount of water and flooding, the downed trees and debris, and the loss of electricity, New York City and its surrounding areas looked as if they had gone ten rounds in the ring and come out on the losing end.

Amidst the first few drops of rain, a building collapsed in Chelsea, completely unrelated to the storm, but still requiring the assistance of Civil Service employees. Our esteemed civil workers did their best to maintain the safety and integrity of the people and the surrounding areas within range of the damaged building. By 9:30 pm, the Hudson River was flowing into Ground Zero, Carey Tunnel, and the New York City Subway Tunnels, halting underground transportation for days. Jane's Carousel, in the Dumbo area looked like a large and colorful raft adrift at sea, for there was not an inch of land to be seen around it. By 10:30 pm, things took a definite turn for the worse when NYU Hospital lost power, and the back up generator failed to engage. Hundreds of injured and sick patients needed to be safely evacuated to neighboring hospitals amidst the outside chaos. Around eleven that evening, residents of the city, out of desperation, took to calling 911 for a variety of reasons, such as downed branches, lack of power, and flooding issues, thereby angering the city Mayor.

The following morning brought more sights of destruction, but thankfully, Sandy was on her way out. First responders, including the Sanitation Department of New York, threw themselves into their work, moving large amounts of downed tree branches and debris, working twelve hour shifts amidst chaotic and dangerous areas, and helping the residents of the city slowly begin to rebuild their lives. The Pandora's Box had finally been closed.

1. Why did New York and its surrounding areas look as if they came out on the losing end of a boxing match?

    a) There was water everywhere

    b) The city was without power

    c) There was debris everywhere

d) All of the above

2. Select the best description of the order of events that were a direct result of Hurricane Sandy.

    a) NYU Hospital lost power, 911 was inundated with calls, the subway flooded, and a building fell

    b) The building in Chelsea fell, The Hudson overflowed, NYU lost power, and 911 was inundated with calls

    c) The subway flooded, the building in Chelsea fell, and 911 was overwhelmed with calls

    d) The Hudson River overflowed, NYU Hospital lost power, and 911 was overwhelmed with calls

3. Why would one assume Mayor of the city was upset with the residents?

    a) He felt that they weren't doing enough to help out during the storm

    b) They were calling 911 for non-life threatening situations, tying up the emergency line.

    c) They were becoming frantic over minor situations

    d) They were exaggerating the severity of the storm

4. Complete the following sentence: "In an emergency situation, first responders must _____"

    a) "must decide who's in charge of what area, and act accordingly."

    b) "must work together in a concentrated effort to provide relief to those affected."

    c) "must call 911."

    d) "must check with the Mayor before proceeding with any assistance."

5. In the first paragraph, what can one assume a Pandora's Box contains?

    a) A well to contain excess water

    b) A box full of troubles and problems

    c) Tools to help those in need

    d) A box of emergency flares

Questions 6 through 12 should be answered SOLELY on the information contained in the following passage.

Collection of residential refuse, recyclables and residential bulk is provided free to the residents of New York City by the DSNY. Local law 19 of 1989 designates that certain materials must be separated at the source (residence, school or office building) and placed in receptacles separate from refuse in order to be delivered to a recycling facility. The recycling program, which started in 1986, is an important part of the Department of Sanitation's operation. The primary goal is to reduce waste, reuse goods, and lessen our carbon footprint on this planet. Mandated recyclable materials include paper and cardboard, metal and glass, plastics, and bulky items such as furniture or appliances. There was also an initiative for "Leaf and Yard Waste Collection" that aimed to use waste such as food scraps as an asset to enrich soil; that program is still in effect, but in limited areas.

Composting is a natural process that turns organic materials in to a rich soil, providing the earth with necessary nutrients and soil microbes that aid plant growth. Due to budget cuts, however, the program has been suspended until further notice, except for the pilot group of residential homes that were initially involved with the Organics Collection project. As it stands, leaves and yard waste are again set curbside in opaque garbage bags; no paper lawn and leaf bags may be used during the suspension.

Paper items that can be recycled include newspapers, magazines, catalogues, and cardboard boxes. These items maybe bound with twine or clear tape and set curbside, or can be placed in a bin marked with green recycling decals. When it comes to metal and glass, cartons and plastics, these items are to be placed in a clear plastic bag, or any bin labeled with blue recycling decals. Proper etiquette would be to rinse out any excess liquid prior to placing items in the bag, simply to save paper items like cartons from being saturated so that they may remain recyclable.

Furniture and appliances are referred to as Bulky Items. These encompass refrigerators, air conditioners, plastic furniture and the like. Certain items in this category may contain chlorofluorocarbon gas, or freon, and if this is the case, the resident would need to make a phone call to 311 so that the harmful gases are removed prior to the item being recycled. It is also important to note that for safety reasons, all doors must be removed from freezers and refrigerators before being placed at the curb.

New York City residents have been doing their part in assisting the city with their recycling efforts, achieving a rate of 15.4% in the city's 2014 diversion rate. Hopefully, with more diligent care, that number will continue to rise in the coming years and reach the projected goal of 20% in 2015.

6. What is the principle behind New York City's recycling initiative

    a) To have stricter rules for garbage collection

    b) To lessen waste and be more conscious of what can be reuse

    c) To collect money from businesses and schools

a) To have more trash receptacles

7. Why would you assume the "Leaf and Yard Waste Collection" program would benefit the city?

   a) It would lessen the mess of throwing leaves and yard waste in with the regular trash

   b) It would provide the city with extra garbage to achieve its goal

   c) It would nourish the soil, providing plants and seeds with a fertile growth environment

   d) It would help residents do less yard work

8. What color decal would one find on the paper goods receptacle?

   a) Red

   b) White

   c) Blue

   d) Green

9. Why might one want to rinse out glass bottles and containers before placing them in a clear bag?

   a) To keep paper cartons in their best shape in order to be recycled

   b) To keep the sanitation worker clear of hazardous material

   c) To keep the liquids from spilling all over the street

   d) To keep raccoons from getting into the garbage and drinking liquids

10. Which of these items would merit a call to 311 prior to being placed curbside?

    a) A wooden rocking chair

    b) A plastic file cabinet

    c) A small air conditioner

    d) Ten pairs of old and worn shoes

11. What is the logic behind removing the doors of freezers and refrigerators prior to leaving these items at the curb?

    a) They are too awkward to manage while they are attached

    b) The metal hinges affect the recycling process

    c) Someone may slam their finger during the removal process

d) As a safety precaution, to keep a child from climbing inside and getting trapped.

12. Which of the following sentences is true, according to the above passage?

    a) Local Law 19 of 1989 states that garbage must be separated

    b) The "Leaf and Yard Collection" program is still in full effect today.

    c) Furniture and appliances are called "Bulky Categories"

    d) New York City achieved a recycling rate of 15.4% in 2014, and aims to raise that number in 2015.

Answer questions 13-19 SOLELY on the basis of the following passage.

The Asian Longhorned Beetle (ALB) is an invasive beetle that is native to China, yet cities across the United States are suffering damages from its ill effects. The ALB feeds on wood, and tunnelling by its larvae damages the vascular system of trees. Continued attacks will lead to a halt in tree crown growth, inhibiting new branches and leaves from forming and eventually, the tree will die.

The Asian Longhorned Beetle is believed to have arrived here in the States via untreated packing crates and wooden pallets that originated in China. Infestations have been discovered in all five boroughs of New York City, as well as parts of Long Island. The ALB has also been documented as causing tree damage in parts of Ohio, Chicago, New Jersey and Massachusetts. The beetles favor a variety of trees, more specifically the horsechestnut, the willow, elm, birch, poplar and ash. They move swiftly through the tree bark and can quickly infect an entire tree lined street. The only effective means of controlling the spread of the ALB is to remove the infested trees and destroy them via chipping or burning. The earlier the infestation is found, the quicker the tree can be removed, thereby aiding in the eradication of the beetle.

There are several signs that point to beetle infestation of a tree. Initially, one might see small round or oval holes; female beetles chew oval holes and deposit one egg in each pit. Another sign to look for is an accumulation of sawdust amongst the branches that meet the main trunk of the tree. This can indicate that the larvae have hatched and are burrowing through the bark. Occasionally, one may also see oozing sap combined with clumps of coarse sawdust on various branches. This is another sign of trauma occurring within the tree, and certainly points to an ALB infestation

As a result of the damaging effects of this beetle, a quarantine regulating the movement of tree wood was placed over the boroughs of Brooklyn, Manhattan, Queens and Staten Island. The New York City Parks Department made a concentrated effort to personally examine every batch of wood or tree pruning that was to be set out as garbage. Residents were instructed to call 311 prior to taking out any wood debris, and a date and time of collection was given. Due to their diligence, the quarantine in Manhattan and Staten Island was lifted on May 14, 2013. Hopefully, in due time, the other boroughs will be beetle free and new trees will be planted so that they may flourish along the streets once more.

13. From the above passage, one can deduce that "quarantine" means:

   a) an illness that is dangerous to many

   b) To separate and restrict the movement of persons or items

   c) A private area where people can enter and then leave freely

   d) A rule that is put in place to assist in recycling collection

14. How did the Asian Longhorned Beetle end up in the United States?

   a) It is originally from Ohio

   b) It was in a crate that came from Hong Kong

   c) It was in untreated wood that originated in China

   d) It spread from the trees of Long Island

15. What do oval holes and sawdust around the main trunk of a tree indicate?

   a) Larvae have hatched and are eating their way through the wood.

   b) Construction was occurring nearby

   c) A woodpecker has been pecking away at the tree

   d) Inspectors have come around to take samples of the tree sap

16. What best explains the cause of death for a tree infested with ALB?

   a) The beetle chews through the bark and turns it into sawdust.

   b) The beetle eats away at the leaves until the tree dies

   c) The beetle eats away at the inside of the tree and stops new growth from occurring, causing the tree to die

   d) Trees die when their sap starts to leak

17. Which tree variety is a favorite of the ALB?

   a) The maple tree

   b) The spruce tree

   c) The cherry tree

   d) The elm tree

18. Which statement is false?

    a) The quarantine in the Bronx has been lifted.

    b) The beetle originates from China

    c) The only was to remove an infested tree is by chipping or burning

    d) Beetles can stop tree crown growth, leading to the death of the tree

19. What are city residents required to do for their wood and tree pruning debris?

    a) To call the Sanitation Department for an appointment

    b) To burn it in a barrel in their backyard

    c) To call 311 for a date given by the Parks Department to put it out curbside on recycling days.

Chapter 1: Written & Reading Comprehension

Answers for questions 1 -19

1. d
2. d
3. b
4. b
5. b
6. b
7. c
8. d
9. a
10. c
11. d
12. a
13. b
14. c
15. a
16. c
17. d
18. a
19. c

Chapter 2: PROBLEM SENSITIVITY

20. Why is vehicle pre-inspection important?

    a) So that you can report vehicle problems to your supervisor

    b) To prevent vehicle accidents

    c) To ensure that vehicle is operating efficiently in order to prevent vehicle breakdowns

    d) All of the above

21. During your time in the field, in order to help prevent vehicle breakdowns you should:

    a) Monitor gauges to make sure that they are within acceptable ranges

    b) Check tire pressure

    c) Check headlight operation

    d) None of the above

22. When returning vehicle to garage, part of priority vehicle inspection route should be:

    a) Inspect windshield wipers

    b) Check condition of tires, rims and lug nuts

    c) Check for proper coolant level in radiator

    d) All of the above

23. If a broken main leaf spring is discovered during pre-trip inspection, you should:

    a) Report problem to supervisor upon returning vehicle to garage at the end of the day

    b) Disregard until at least one-fourth of springs are broken

    c) Report problem immediately so that the vehicle will be placed "out of service"

    d) None of the above

24. An example of exhaust system defect is:

    a) Backfire noises out of tailpipe

b) Condensation leaking out of exhaust system

c) Exhaust system parts that are rubbing against fuel system parts

d) All of the above

25. After engine is started:

    a) Oil pressure should be normal within seconds

    b) Warning lights and buzzers should go off right away

    c) Ammemeter/voltmeter should be in normal range

    d) All of the above

26. Part of 'Right side" vehicle inspection is:

    a) Make sure reflectors are clean and proper color

    b) Tank contains fuel

    c) Make sure passenger side restraint system is working properly

    d) Mark sure right turn signal is operating

27. Parking brake inspection includes:

    a) Place vehicle into low gear

    b) Pump brake pedal three times

    c) Check brake fluid level

    d) None of the above

28. Which of the following is not part of double-clutching:

    a) Release clutch

    b) Push in clutch and shift to higher gear simultaneously

    c) Release clutch and press accelerator simultaneously

    d) Push in clutch and press acceleration simultaneously

29. The best way to determining engine speed is:

    a) Listen to engine noise

    b) Compare speed stated on speedometer with what gear you are in

    c) Look at the tachometer

    d) None of the above

30. Which of the following is most effective in reducing break wear and slowing down:

    a) Pumping on brake pedal

    b) Down-shifting

    c) Using "retarders" at the appropriate time

    d) None of the above

31. Which of the following is true:

    a) Poor traction on drive wheels does not affect retarder performance

    b) Poor traction on drive wheels increases performance of retarders

    c) When there is poor traction on drive wheels, retarders should be turned off

    d) Poor traction of front wheels affects retarders more than anything else

32. The most important factors when stopping are:

    a) Driver alertness and weather conditions

    b) Condition of tires and brakes

    c) Transmission and engine performance

    d) None of the above

33. The principal method of reducing speed on down grades is:

    a) Pumping brakes

    b) Up-shifting near the governed RPM's

    c) Down-shifting near the governed RPM'S Combined with proper braking technique

    d) Down-shifting only

34. Which of the following is the best way to deal with tailgaters:

    a) Increase speed

    b) Reduce speed abruptly

    c) Change lanes

    d) Avoid quick changes when turning or slowing down

35. When you start your shift your supervisor tells your assignments for that day. You do not understand some of the things he mentioned. What is the first step to try and solve this dilemma?

a) Ask one of your coworkers for help.

b) Just try to do whatever you think he meant and then when you're all done at the end of your shift ask him if you did everything correctly.

c) Ask your supervisor to repeat slowly and clearly what he would like you to do.

d) Just do the best you can and whatever you understood that he wants you to do.

True or False

36. One of the purposes of the suspension system is to keep axles in place.

37. Leaking shock absorbers are not serious enough to place vehicle "out of service".

38. Excess fumes leaking into the cab is not serious enough of a problem to place it "out of service".

39. After starting engine, air pressure should build between 50-90 PSI within 30 seconds.

40. When pulled over to the side of the road, drivers can crash into the rear of your parked vehicle unless you have both the emergency flashers and tail lights on.

41. Pumping brakes to check for hydraulic leaks is not part of brake inspection.

42. Vehicle positioning is necessary in order to ensure backing out properly.

43. Engine RPM is never a factor in determining what proper gear to be in when shifting.

44. Pressing accelerator during down shifting is not part of the down shifting process.

45. Total stopping distance includes: perception distance, reaction distance, braking distance.

Chapter 2: Problem Sensitivity
Answers for questions 20 - 45

20. d
21. a
22. b
23. c
24. c
25. d
26. b
27. a
28. d
29. c
30. c
31. c
32. a
33. c
34. d
35. c
36. TRUE
37. FALSE
38. FALSE
39. FALSE
40. TRUE
41. FALSE
42. TRUE
43. FALSE
44. FALSE
45. TRUE

Chapter 3: Written Expression

Questions 46-53 are to be answered solely on the information given in the description and table below.

Your regular working hours are 7 AM until 3:30 PM, Monday through Friday. Your lunch area is half an hour (mandatory you take it, if you work 4 hours or more). Your weekend shift begins at 7 AM. Any and all hours you work on the weekend will be paid as overtime rate. Your regular hourly rate is $20.00. Your overtime rate is $30.00.

Date	Log in	Log Out	O/T	STRAIGHT RATE	OT RATE	TOTAL HOURS	TOTAL GROSS PAY
Monday		1530	3				
Tuesday	0700		0				
Wednesday	0700	1530	1				
Thursday	0700	A	B		C		$250.00
Friday	0700	1530	4				F
Saturday		1200	4				D
Sunday							
		TOTAL	E				G

46. How much will your Gross pay be for Friday (select what belongs in F)?

    a) $280.00

    b) $140.00

    c) $120.00

    d) $270.00

47. How much will your total Gross pay be for this week (select what belongs in G)?

    a) $700.00

    b) $1385.00

    c) $1160.00

    d) $1210.00

SANITATION WORKER EXAM PREP BOOK

48. Which day did you earn the most?

    a) Sunday

    b) Thursday

    c) Saturday

    d) Friday

49. How much did you earn for the weekend (select what belongs in D)?

    a) $240.00

    b) $80.00

    c) $105.00

    d) $255.00

50. What is the total amount of hours of overtime you worked this week (select what belongs in E)?

    a) 15

    b) 12

    c) 19

    d) 0

51. Select what belongs in **B** on your timesheet

    a) 1

    b) 3

    c) 16:00

    d) 7

52. Select what belongs in **C**:

    a) $60.00

    b) $140.00

    c) $95.00

    d) $90.00

53. Did you work a full day or half-day on Saturday?

    a) Full

b) Half

54. Which sentence makes most sense?

   a) The typical sanitation truck for residential waste can hold 25 cubic yards of waste.

   b) The typical sanitation truck can hold 25 cubic yards of residential waste.

Questions 55-58 are to be answered solely on the basis of the information given in the passage below.

Driving while texting, haz become a leading cause of moter vehicle accidents. Talking on a cellphone has alsoe became a big problem, and is a cauz of motor vehicle axidents. in order to fix this situation, the locale authoritees in Many states have creeted new and very strict laws. Driver reaction time wile txting or talking on a cellphone is increased, and theirfore new lawz are constantly being put intoo force all round the country (In order to reeduce the number of motor vehicle acidents).

55. How many grammatical errors are there in this passage?

   a) 1

   b) 19

   c) 13

   d) 21

56. Are there any errors in the second line? If so, how many?

   a) None

   b) 4

   c) 2

57. Are there any errors in the second to last line? If so, how many?

   a) 2

   b) None

   c) 4

58. How many punctuation marks are missing?

    a) 1

    b) 2

    c) 6

    d) 5

Questions 59-62 are to be answered solely on the information given in the description and passage below.

Incident Facts

Time of accident: 6:30 am

Vehicles Involved: Sanitation Truck, 2010 Black Chevy Suburban

Names of Sanitation Workers in Sanitation truck: Giovanni, Hector

2010 Black Chevy Suburban: Mary Concord

Mary Concord's Lawyer: Albert Cohn

Mary Concord's Birthdate: August 15, 1960

Mary Concord's Employer: Abc Company

Giovanni's Lawyer: Trent Larney

Giovanni's Birthdate: March 18, 1970

Hector's Lawyer: Maria Lamonent

Hector's Birthdate: November 7, 1981

Weather Conditions: 25 Degrees Farenheit, Just Began To Snow

Sanitation Workers' Supervisor's Name: Leroy Wilkins

Sanitation workers Giovanni and Hector were on their normally scheduled route in the Tremont area of the Bronx. It was 6:30 am, they were on Baychester Avenue heading north. It had just begun to snow. They were pulling over to the right to stop and pick up from the public school (parallel to parked cars). A woman driving a 2010 Black Chevy Suburban was approaching them from the opposite direction (it was a two-way street). She tried to squeeze between the parked cars on her right and the sanitation truck on her left. Giovanni was in the back of the truck dumping the cans into the chute when she hit his left arm (he was injured, but not seriously).

- A Notify their supervisor immediately
- B Fill out a Sanitation Dept. Incident report
- C Fill out a police report
- D Call 911
- E Ambulance takes Giovanni to the hospital

59. What would be the logical next steps that should occur and in the correct order?

    a) A,D,E,C,B

    b) D,E,A,C,B

    c) D,A,E,C,B

60. What information is NOT important to be noted on the police report?

    a) Model and make of the vehicles involved

    b) Time of incident

    c) Mary Concord's Auto insurance company's information

    d) Mary Concord's Lawyer's contact information

    e) Birthdates of all involved

    f) Weather conditions

61. If Supervisor Wilkins asks Giovanni for a quick sketch of what occurred, which one would be correct?

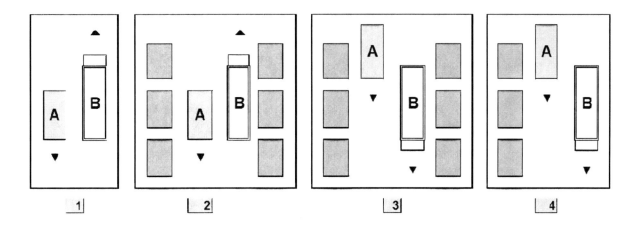

Hector needs to call 911 to get an ambulance to the scene because Giovanni got hurt.

62. Which of the following statements would be the most effective way to communicate this point to the 911 dispatch operator?

    a) My friend Giovanni is hurt please send ambulance.

    b) This crazy woman hit my friend Giovanni when he was unloading trash in the back of the truck. She hit his left hand and it's bleeding.

    c) Hi, I'm with the Sanitation department, there was an accident. No one is seriously hurt, but my coworker will need medical attention and an ambulance.

    d) Need an ambulance right away.

You decide to go on vacation with your family Memorial Weekend 2015. The dates of the flights you would like to take are : May 23-May 30. You only work Monday through Fridays. You need to fill out a Vacation request form so you can get your Supervisor's approval.

VACATION REQUEST FORM

Date:	A	Approved by Supervisor:	Yes No D	
Employee:	B	Start Date:	E	
Department:	C	End Date:	F	
Requesting J days off - paid				
Supervisor Signature G		Date H		
I understand that until both my Supervisor signs this form, my vacation request is not approved.				
Employee's Signature I				

63. How many days of work will you miss (select what belongs in J)

    a) 8

    b) 4

    c) 5

    d) 6

64. What belongs in E?

    a) May 23

    b) May 26

    c) May 25

    d) May 24

65. What belongs in F?

    a) June 1

    b) May 30

    c) May 31

    d) May 29

Chapter 3: Written Expression

Answers for questions 46 -65

46. a   8hrs x $20=$160, 4hrs x $30=$120, $160+$120 = $280
47. b $250 + $160 + $190 + $250 + $280 + $255 = $1385
48. d   Friday, $280
49. d   9hrs - .5hr for lunch = 8.5 hrs , 8.5hrs x $30 = $255(weekend rate is $30/hr)
50. a   3 + 1 + 3 + 4 + 4 = 15 hrs
51. b   see explanation at the bottom of this page for questions 51 and 52
52. d
53. b
54. b
55. b
56. b
57. c
58. d
59. c
60. d
61. 2
62. c
63. b
64. b
65. a

Corrected paragraph for questions 55-58: Driving while texting, has become a leading cause of motor vehicle accidents. Talking on a cellphone has also become a big problem, and is a cause of many motor vehicle accidents. In order to fix this situation, the local authorities in many states have created new and very strict laws. Driver reaction time while texting or talking on a cellphone increases. New laws are constantly being put into force all around the country in order to reduce the number of motor vehicle accidents.

For questions 63-65, remember: Memorial Day is a National Paid Holiday for Civil Service Employees. You will not need to use one of your vacation days.

Questions 51 and 52 EXPLANATION:

You have total amount for that day : $250 (it is noted in the column labeled TOTAL GROSS PAY for Thursday) Step 2: 8hrs x $20=$160. Step 3: $250-$160=$90(this amount belongs in C). Step 4: $90/ $30= 3 hrs of overtime (this amount belongs in B)

Chapter 4: INFORMATION ORDERING

Scenario: Ambulance just arrived at the scene of an accident between a sanitation truck and a passenger car. The driver of the car is lying on the ground. The paramedics think he might have a back injury.

The following steps are taken in order to place the victim on the backboard.

1. If the victim is not lying on the center, they need to slide him to the center of the backboard.
2. They should roll the victim onto the backboard.
3. They should position the backboard on the ground right next to the victim.
4. They should roll the victim on his side so that the backboard can be placed underneath him.

66. Which is the correct order?

    a) 3, 1, 4, 2

    b) 1, 4, 3, 2

    c) 3, 4, 2, 1

    d) 4, 3 ,2, 1

67. 20 , 30 , 25 , 35 , 30, ...

    a) add 10, add 5

    b) add 10, subtract 5

    c) add 5, add 10

    d) add 5, subtract 10

68. 27 , 23 , 19 , 15 , 11 , ...

    a) Subtract 3

    b) Subtract 5

    c) Subtract 4

    d) Subtract 2

Use numbers 2 , 63 , 45 (put numbers in the correct order, in the blanks below:)

69. __ X __ - __ =81

   a) 45 , 2 , 63

   b) 63 , 2 , 45

Use numbers 52 , 7 , 5, 91

70. __ / __ + __ x __ = 325

   a) 91 , 7 , 52 , 5

   b) 91 , 5 , 52 , 7

Use numbers 4 , 35 , 68

71. __ - __ + __ = 99

   a) 68, 4, 35

   b) 4, 35, 68

For questions 72 - 75 , what are the missing numbers in the sequence (hint: look for the pattern)?

72. 16 , 22 , 34 , 52 , 76 ……

   a) Add 6

   b) There is no pattern

   c) Multiples of 6

   d) Add 12

73. 100 , 106 , 112 , 118…

   a) Add 6

   b) Multiples of 6

   c) There is no pattern

   d) Deduct 6

74. 0.4 , 0.5 , 0.7 , 1.0 ….

   a) 1.1

   b) 1.2

   c) 1.3

   d) 1.4

For questions 75 - 80 , arrange the words in a sentence (in the most logical order)

75. snow / streets/ provides/ collect/ the Sanitation Dept./ services/ main/ the / four/ waste/ recycle/ clean/ clear/ removal/ are

76. waste/ one/ composting/ on-site/ minimize/ to/ is/ way

77. per/ pounds/ waste/ household/ 41/ week/ generated/ per/ is/ of

78. 11 tons/ glass/ plastic/ trucks/ carry/ 10 tons/ containers/ metal/ of/ recycling/ and

79. waste/ trucks/ commercial/ 15 tons/ carry/ collection/ up to/ can/ of

80. create/ source/ used/ can/ landfill gas/ energy/ of/ electricity/ to/ used/ as/ a/ be/ of

81. Which of the following statements is in the correct grammatical order:

    a) You're supposed to not throw rechargeable batteries in the trash.

    b) You're not supposed to throw batteries in the trash.

82. Which of the following statements is in the correct grammatical order:

    a) I think I and you need to have a meeting.

    b) I think you and I need to have a meeting.

Chapter 4: INFORMATION ORDERING

Answers for questions 66 -82

66. c
67. b   Add 10, Subtract 5 : 20,30 (+10) 30, 25 (-5) ....
68. c   Subtract 4 : 27, 23 (-4) 23, 19 (-4) ....
69. b (63 x 2 = 126   126 - 45 = 81)
70. a (91 / 7=13   13+52=65   65 x 5= 325)
71. a (68 - 4 = 64   64 + 35 = 99)
72. c (multiples of 6 : 16+6=22   22+12=34   34+18-52   52+24=76)
73. a (pattern is to add 6 to each number: 100+6=106   106+6=112   112+6=118)
74. d (answer can be solved by: +.1, + .2, + .3, + .4)
75. The four main services the Sanitation Dept. provides are clean streets, collect waste, recycle and clear snow.
76. On-site composting is one way to minimize waste.
77. 41 pounds per week of waste is generated per household.
78. Recycling trucks carry 11 tons of paper or 10 tons of metal, glass and plastic containers.
79. Commercial waste collection trucks can carry up to 15 tons of waste.
80. Landfill gas can be used as a source of energy to create electricity.
81. b
82. b

SANITATION WORKER EXAM PREP BOOK

Chapter 5: DEDUCTIVE REASONING

Answer question 83-90 SOLELY based on the following passage.

The streets of New York City were veritably teeming with garbage in the late 19th century. The filth in the streets was so profound, that it was not uncommon for children to be playing shin deep in manure and muck, while the adults walked to and fro in their daily activities, the food waste and sludge sticking to their clothing and following them mercilessly. Why couldn't the city be cleaned? The politicians in Tammany Hall refused to put money into this endeavor and would tell anyone who would listen that city cleanup was an impossible feat, that New York City was too dense, too populated for any real difference to be noted, not pointing out that Boston and Philadelphia were also densely populated but were still able to clean their city streets.

When a corruption scandal erupted in the early 1890's, Tammany politicians were kicked out of office and a new Mayor took over the reigns. William Strong came into office and vowed to clean the city, starting with the police department's corruption and ending with the filthy streets of the city. Teddy Roosevelt was selected to reform the police department, but it took the Mayor a bit of time before settling on the appropriate person for street clean up. He finally settled on George Waring, a sanitary engineer and retired Civil War major. Waring had a history with the city, having been appointed as an agricultural and drainage engineer for Central Park back in 1857. At that time, much of Central Park was wetlands; it was under his supervision and design that led to the construction of the various lakes and ponds of the park that exist today. He was also a great help to the city of Memphis, Tennessee; in 1878, yellow fever swept through Memphis, due in part to the standing water that was everywhere. Waring was sent to assist the town and he set about designing a better sewage and drainage system, which the town implemented. Streets were cleaner and, as a result, yellow fever became a thing of the past for Memphis.

In 1895, Waring was appointed commissioner of the city's Department of Street Cleaning, and began making drastic changes that are still in place today. He started by giving structure to the job, for example, one street sweeper was responsible for cleaning 3rd Avenue for a total of ten blocks deep, and should be done within an eight hour parameter, while a cart worker followed that sweeper during that same time frame. Officers were responsible for each crew, and those officers themselves reported to a higher-up who ultimately reported to Waring. It was a military-like structure that displeased the members of the crew, yet it worked surprisingly well. After establishing this system, he sent crews to the poorest neighborhoods of the city, which were also the filthiest. The wealthier neighborhoods paid to hire their own cleaners, so those streets were a far sight better than areas teeming with newly arrived immigrants and families searching for work. The first hurdle was to gain acceptance into the poor areas.

People in Five Points would try to attack the clean up crew with sticks, and would often hurl bricks at them to get them to leave. The crews however, kept at it, and after two weeks had won over the people living in the tenements, because now their neighborhood was as clean as any other.

Waring had creative ideas in order to achieve clean streets. He had his sanitation crews wearing white in order to foster an idea of cleanliness and good hygiene, following the thought that doctors wear white, and keep people healthy. He also put them in white helmets, the very same worn by police, to show that they too were figures of authority, and they were given the nickname "The White Wings". The White Wings became the heroes of New York City, turning what was once a foul and waste-ridden area in a clean city. With the rise in clean streets, the rates of both communicable diseases, as well as mortality went down. Unfortunately, he died at the end of his third year of service, after ironically contracting yellow fever in Cuba. In Waring's three years at the helm, he made a huge impact on the city, with his ideas being a tremendous contribution to the inhabitants of New York. As a sign of gratitude, Waring Avenue in the North Bronx was named in his honor. Tammany Hall politicians had said it couldn't be done; thankfully, Waring proved them wrong.

83. How could the above passage best be summarized?

    a) 19th century New York City was a tough place to live

    b) The politicians of Tammany Hall assisted Waring in his efforts to clean up the city.

    c) George Waring's implementation of a novel approach to the cleaning of New York City streets

    d) Corruption was a huge factor in the filthiness of the city

84. What could be a reason that Tammany Hall politicians refused to initiate clean up efforts for the city?

    a) They thought efforts would be useless because New York was too heavily populated

    b) Clean up would require money and a plan, an effort Tammany Hall refused to invest in

    c) The police commissioner refused to allow them to start clean up efforts

    d) Clean up was not part of their job description

85. What quality best made Waring an ideal candidate for the job at hand?

    a) He was a Major in the military and was well acquainted with giving orders

b) His prior efforts at assisting Central Park's drainage issues

   c) He wasn't afraid of standing up to politicians

   d) He helped Memphis, Tennessee with their sewer drainage system, thereby keeping the streets clean and lowering rates of illness

86. Why could one assume the people of Five Points were initially angry to see the clean up crews in their neighborhood?

   a) Police corruption had led to a deep distrust of any and all city employees

   b) They felt that they were being blamed for their neighborhood's lack of cleanliness

   c) They were attacked first, so they needed to defend themselves against the crew

   d) They were being forced to clean up their neighborhood without any assistance

87. What best explains why the clean up crews were initially displeased with Waring and his new initiative?

   a) He was making them work eight hour days

   b) Everything was regimented with military precision, and workers were being held accountable for their work

   c) They did not like wearing white

   d) Their clean up route was too long for an eight hour work day

88. What did Waring feel that uniforms for the White Wings crew would accomplish?

   a) The workers would take pride in their job

   b) Workers would have a sense of unity

   c) The people of New York City would view them as persons of authority, much like the police officers

   d) Uniforms would keep their clothing clean

89. How did Waring assist the city of Memphis?

   a) He helped manage their clean up crew

   b) He implemented a new system of street cleaning

   c) He designed a better waste and drainage system to keep streets clean

d) He killed all the mosquitos that transmitted yellow fever

90. Select the best order of events from the choices below:

a) Waring was appointed commissioner of the Department of Sanitation, helped Memphis combat yellow fever, assisted in Central Park's drainage system, and died in 1898.

b) Waring assisted Memphis to combat yellow fever, helped address Central Park's drainage system, became commissioner in 1898, and died three years later. Waring was first appointed commissioner, assisted in Central Park's drainage system, helped combat yellow fever in Memphis, and died in 1898.

c) Waring worked on Central Park's drainage system, helped combat yellow fever in Memphis, was appointed commissioner, and then died in 1898.

Answer questions 91-97 SOLELY on the basis of the following passage:

Sustainable farming practices have been around since mid 2300 B.C., with the Akkadian Empire using manure within their agricultural practices in the Mesopotamian Valley. Clay tablets found from that time period show images of the farmers spreading manure and organic matter through fields and tending to the soil by watering and turning it before planting their seeds. During the 18th to 19th century, the United States had such a tremendous amount of untoiled land that was rich with nutrients that farmers disregarded the idea of sustainable farming practices. The idea of composting meant time and planning, and although it would benefit them in the long term, they felt that it was not a step they needed to take just yet. On and on they farmed their rich land, until they finally depleted all the necessary nutrients that would yield a substantial crop. By the middle of the nineteenth century, the decrease of crop production led farmers to explore more sustainable ways to farm. The idea of composting again reared its head, and the farmers slowly began to use organic waste produced on their farms as a means to replenish and maintain soil fertility. The growth in urban city population also fostered a means to facilitate composting. The organic waste from cities such as Philadelphia and New York was transported to farms in order to be used as fertilizer. Over the course of time, however, these city populations continued to grow at a massive rate, and the demand of farmed produce simply could not be met by the farmers that were using compost as a natural fertilizer. In addition to that, recycling became much more difficult as more and more people continued to move into the city. The sheer density of the population made storing organic waste a trial, especially if pick up was to occur in four days time; people did not want these odors lingering by their homes and, little by little, the desire to recycle organic waste began to dwindle before coming to a standstill.

In 1918, after World War I had ended, the government had a surplus of nitrogen that was initially to be used for explosives. Upon the war's end, they sent this excess to the agricultural industry, and synthetic nitrogen began to be used as an inexpensive form of artificial fertilizer. Farmers were urged to use artificial fertilizer in order to meet the demands of the growing urban population, and to eliminate food shortages. Unbeknownst to both farmers and government, these artificial fertilizers substantially deteriorated the quality of the soil, and by the early 1920's farmers were once again guided to the practice of organic matter being used as fertilizer. Upon the heels of this decision, the East Coast suffered what has come to be known as the Dust Bowl, an environmental disaster that ravaged the southern Plains in the early 1930's. Farmers, lured by the prices of wheat, plowed up millions of acres of natural grass in order to plant wheat in as many areas of land as possible. At this point, The Great Depression had struck, and with it, a drought that proceeded to turn the oceans of wheat into dried husks. The soil, without any grass to act as an anchor, was lifted up and dust clouds were formed, some as high as 10,000 feet, and as long as two miles. It took many years for farmers to recover from that disaster, and it affected the population of the plains as well, with many people moving from their homes and heading toward major cities.

Every ten years or so, discussion again turns to composting as a solution for the troubles that have befallen our agricultural system. Currently, waste management in New York City has become a crucial topic, more so since their primary source of waste disposal, the Fresh Kills landfill that was located in Staten Island, closed down in 2001. The Department of Sanitation launched a Backyard Composting Pilot project to investigate the possibility of implementing a large-scale backyard-composting project in New York. The results of the pilot program revealed that there were not enough New Yorkers who had access to backyards and interest in composting was limited, at best. The Sanitation Department also conducted a research project that involved the collection of 500 tons of mixed waste that was sent to Massachusetts to be sorted. The results were that this was indeed a viable option, producing compost of worthy value, but the intense screening of the waste would lead to immense costs.

Composting is a tried and true method of producing a natural fertilizer for soil. As yet, however, there has not been a viable and cost efficient manner with which to procure organic waste on a grand scale. Urban areas have the disadvantage of being short on space in order to house a composting plant, and when transporting tons of waste to areas further out, cost again becomes a factor. For now New York City maintains pilot programs such as "Grow NYC" and small sample areas that continue to use composting bins in their private homes , but one hope that in due time, a solution will be found that will allow a feasible and viable form of composting to occur on a much grander scale in an urban setting.

91. The above passage is best summarized by:

   a) Fertilizer is critical to farming

   b) It is clear that organic waste is the best fertilizer, but it is difficult, time consuming, and expensive to obtain

c) Artificial fertilizers deplete the soil of nutrients

d) Farmers gave up farming after the Dust Bowl in the 1930's.

92. In the passage, why were farmers urged to use nitrogen in their fields?

    a) The government didn't need to make any more explosives

    b) It was good for the soil

    c) It produced a higher crop yield so that there would be no food shortages

    d) It was the only method of fertilization available

93. Why did it become difficult to collect organic waste from urban areas in the mid 1900's?

    a) The population was too dense, and nobody wanted the waste lingering outside their doorsteps until collection day.

    b) People did not want to be bothered with saving organic waste

    c) It cost too much to save the waste until pick up day

    d) There were no farms within the city limits

94. What, as stated in the passage, caused the Dust Bowl in the early 1930's?

    a) The Great Depression

    b) Farmers plowed millions of acres of grass and the soil had nothing to hold onto so it was carried by the wind for miles

    c) The drought dried up the land

    d) The farmers didn't give the crops enough water

95. What were the results of the Department of Sanitations Backyard Composting Pilot Program?

    a) Residents loved the idea, but did not have enough time to devote towards collection

    b) It was too expensive for the residents to buy compost bins in their yards

    c) Most residents did not have access to a yard, nor did they exhibit any interest in composting

    d) The smell of composting turned them against the idea

96. What event prompted a fresh look into waste management for the city of New York?

    a) A lack of fertilizer for neighboring farms

b) The Staten Island Fresh Kills landfill closed down in 2001

c) Environmental conservationists worried about the city's carbon footprint

d) A lack of crop production in the Plains

97. What is the biggest stumbling block for composting on a grander scale?

    a) There simply is not enough garbage

    b) People are unwilling to recycle

    c) There is not enough space in an urban setting, and the cost becomes too high when transporting waste out of the area

    d) The government will not back the initiative

Chapter 5: DEDUCTIVE REASONING

Answers for questions 83 -97

83. c
84. b
85. d
86. a
87. b
88. c
89. c
90. d
91. b
92. c
93. a
94. b
95. c
96. b
97. c

Chapter 6: SPATIAL ORIENTATION

For questions 98-103, use the map below:

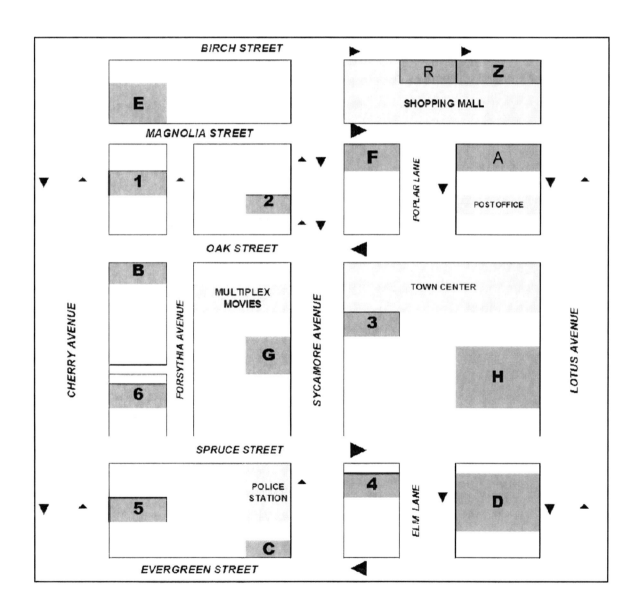

98. Sanitation worker Gerard is on Sycamore Avenue and the Multiplex movies is on his left. He turns left on Oak street, continues one block and turns right on Cherry Avenue. Which location is nearest to him?

    a) 1

    b) E

    c) 6

    d) f

99. Supervisor Rafael is at Z. He calls Gerard and asks him where he is and to pick him up. Gerard is at location 4. What is the most direct route for Gerard to get to his Supervisor's current location?

    a) North on Sycamore Avenue, East on Magnolia Street, North on Birch Street

    b) East on Spruce Street, North on Lotus Avenue

    c) South on Sycamore Avenue, East on Evergreen Avenue, North on Lotus Avenue

    d) North on Sycamore Avenue, East on Birch Street

100. Gerard is currently located at C facing South. Larry is at location E. Larry is _____ of Gerard?

    a) East

    b) South

    c) North

    d) West

101. Supervisor Rafael is right in front of the Post Office (Lotus Ave. side). Larry is right in front of the Police Station (Sycamore Avenue side). How many turns does Larry have to make if he wants to go meet his Supervisor?

    a) 3 or 2, depending which way he takes

    b) 2

    c) 1

    d) 4

102. What location (landmark or letter location), is approximately the center point between Rafael, Larry and Gerard? If Rafael is at 5, Gerard is at 3 and Larry is at Z?

a) 2

b) Town Center

c) F

d) Post Office

103. Assuming that there is one street trash receptacle on each street corner and in front of each landmark and letter location, which Street or Avenue will be the one with the most pick-ups needed?

a) Lotus Avenue

b) Cherry Avenue

c) Sycamore Avenue

d) Spruce Street

Answer questions 105-107 based on your knowledge:

104. If you face North and turn through 360°, what direction will you be facing now?

a) East

b) North

c) South

d) West

105. If the letter P is rotated 180 degrees, which is the resulting figure?

a) P

b) ɑ

c) d

d) ᴘ

106. Pedro and Ted are at the truck depot. Pedro is facing North. Ted is facing East. If Pedro turns clockwise through 180° what angle must Ted turn through to face in the same direction as Pedro?

a) 90° clockwise

b) 180° counterclockwise

c) 180° clockwise

d) 90° counterclockwise

Chapter 6: SPATIAL ORIENTATION

Answers for questions 98-106

98. a
99. a
100. a
101. a
102. a
103. c
104. b
105. c
106. a

Chapter 7: MATHEMATICS

107. In the past three years, Sanitation Dept. used 924,845 tons of salt for snow removal. The first year, Sanitation Dept. used 300,000. The second year Sanitation Dept. used 2,156 less than the first year. The number of tons used in the third year was:

    a) 297,844

    b) 2,156

    c) 597,844

    d) 327,001

108. One of the sanitation trucks measures 10 ft x 10ft x 8 ft. How much volume of waste can this truck hold?

    a) 100 cubic feet

    b) 800 cubic feet

    c) 35 cubic yards

    d) 29 cubic yards

109. Jack's hourly rate as a Sanitation Dept. worker is $27.02. He worked 50 hours this week. For the 10 hours overtime that he worked (over 40 hours), the rate is 'double-time'. How much will his gross paycheck be for this week?

    a) $1080.80

    b) $540.04

    c) $1621.20

    d) $1351.00

110. If Sanitation Dept. has 2 Supervisors assigned per 26 Sanitation Dept. worker, what is the ratio?

    a) 1:52

    b) 2:1

    c) 1:13

    d) 1:2

111. The Sanitation Dept. divides the city into sections/districts. Assuming there are 245 sections/districts, what is the average number of sections per Borough?

   a) 49

   b) 61

   c) 40

   d) 48

112. Truck A is carrying 32 (8.64 tons) cubic yards of salt. Truck B is carrying 7.02 tons of salt. The difference of salt the two trucks are carrying is:

   a) 2 cubic yards(.54 tons)

   b) 1

   c) 1.62 tons

   d) 3

For Question 113, answer should be based on the following information:

Five trucks arrive at the incinerator plant to dump.

- Truck A-2 ¼ tons
- Truck B-2 tons
- Truck C-3 tons
- Truck D-1 ¼ tons
- Truck E-1 ¾ tons

113. How many more tons will the incinerator plant have, after all these trucks finish unloading?

   a) 9 ¼ tons

   b) 10 ¼ tons

   c) 10 tons

   d) 9 ¾ tons

For Questions 114-115, answers should be based solely on this passage:

One winter, there were twelve days that it snowed. The total snow

accumulation was twenty-eight inches. The next winter, there were eight days that it snowed. The total snow accumulation for both winters was forty-seven inches.

114. What was the average snow accumulation per day for the first winter?

    a) 3.0 inches

    b) 2.0 inches

    c) 2.3 inches

    d) 1.9 inches

115. What was the average snow accumulation per day for the second winter?

    a) 2.1 inches

    b) 2.0 inches

    c) 2.4 inches

    d) 3.0 inches

116. Your Supervisor asked you to pick up from an additional location to your already planned route for that day. Typically, you would have enough room for extra trash. You want to confirm that you do before you get there. Your truck holds 25 cubic yards, the additional stop will have 2 cubic yards for you to pick up. Will you be able to fit the extra trash?

    a) Yes

    b) Not enough information is provided

117. Before you start your route for the day, the mileage on the truck is 27,561. At the end of your shift, it is 27,615. How many miles did you travel that day?

    a) 154

    b) 53

    c) 54

    d) 20

118. Your truck currently has 39 gallons of gas. This truck uses one gallon of gas per five miles. How many miles can you drive with the amount of gas you currently have?

    a) 39

b) 195

119. What is the number that is two more than one-tenth of one-fifth of one-half of 3,000?

    a) 33

    b) 50

    c) 1,500

    d) 32

120. Giovanni arrives 10 minutes late for the 2:30 pm training class at the union hall. The class is given every hour on the hour, with the last class beginning at 3:20pm. How long does he have to wait for the next class?

    a) 1 hour

    b) 40 minutes

    c) 20 minutes

    d) 60 minutes

121. Pamela will be taking a Health & Safety training class in 16 days. Today is Tuesday the 21st of October. Which day of the week will her class begin?

    a) Friday 11/7

    b) Friday 11/1

    c) Thursday 11/6

    d) Saturday 11/8

122. On Recycling day, one of the blue bags a resident put out for pick-up on the curb contained: 10 green plastic bottles, 5 green glass bottles, 12 soda cans, 9 blue plastic bottles. What are the chances that a peddler picks just one bottle out of the bag that it will be green?

    a) 2 out of 3

    b) 15 out of 36

    c) 1 out of 3

    d) 3.4

123. Every Friday Bob changes the oil on his truck and every other Friday he also changes the oil filter. It is Friday today and he just changed the oil. How long will it be before he does both on the same day again?

SANITATION WORKER EXAM PREP BOOK

b) 2 weeks

c) 1 month

d) 7 days

124. After a snowstorm, the newspapers reported the following: On Wednesday 8 out of 10 neighborhoods in the Bronx haven't been cleared of snow yet. Thursday half of the remaining affected neighborhoods' streets from Wednesday were cleared. On Friday it snowed again. 20% of the neighborhoods that had been cleared on Thursday now were covered with snow again. Based on these statistics, what percent of the neigborhoods had their streets clean on Friday?

a) 1/3

b) 50%

c) 45%

d) ½

125. In your log book, you filled out how much trash you picked up for this past week. Every day you picked up an average of 5 tons per day. You work Monday through Friday. How much total did you pick up for this week, so you can put that total amount in your log book?

a) 5 tons

b) 35 tons

c) 25 tons

d) 125 tons

Chapter 7: MATHEMATICS

Answers for questions 107 -124

107. d

   First year = 300,000

   Second year = 297,844

   Add First year and Second year = 597,844

   Third year = 924,845 is the total for 3 years , subtract the total for 1st and 2nd year, this will give you the amount for the Third year   924,845 - 597,844 = 327,001

108. b (VOLUME : multiply length x width x height   10 X 10 X 8 = 800)

109. c (40 x $27.02 = $1080.80 , OT hourly rate is 2 x $27.02 = $54.04 , 10 x $54.04 = $540.40, total pay is $1080.80 + $540.40 = $1621.20)

110. c (DIVIDE: 26 supervisors / 2 SW = 13, 1 supervisor per 13 SW, ratio is 1:13)

111. a (DIVISION : 254 districts, 5 Boroughs in NYC 254/5 = 49)

112. c (SUBTRACTION with DECIMALS : 8.64 - 7.02 = 1.62)

113. b (ADDING: 2 ¼, + 2 + 3 + 1 ¼ + 1 ¾ = 10 ¼ tons is the total amount that will be added to the Incinerator plant once all these trucks leave the dumpsite)

114. c (DIVIDE: first winter 12 days total snow 28 inches, 28/12=2.3 inches per day)

115. c (MULTIPLE STEPS: Total snow both winters is 47, first winter is 28, Subtract : 47-28=19 total inches for the second winter. Then DIVIDE: second winter 8 days total snow ,19 inches, 19/8= 2.375 inches per day, if you round the answer it will be 2.4 inches)

116. b (missing information is how much trash your truck currently has)

117. c (SUBTRACTION : 27,615 - 27,561 = 54)

118. b (MULTIPLICATION: 1 gal per 5 miles so for 39 gal: 5 miles x 39 gallons =195 miles you can travel)

119. d (FRACTION TO DECIMAL CONNVERSION, MULTI-STEPS:

   ½ = .5, 1/5 = .2, 1/10 = .1, calculation: 3000 x .5= 1500 x .2=300 x .1 = 30 +2= 32)

120. b (Gio arrives at 2:40 , subtract 3:20-2:40 = 40 minutes he will have to wait)

SANITATION WORKER EXAM PREP BOOK

122. b (total bottles = 36, total green bottles = 15, 15 out of 36)

123. b

124. b

- Wednesday 2 neighborhoods were cleared. 8 were not.

- Thursday 50% of 8 not cleared = 4

- Friday 20% of 4 from Thursday = .8

- total cleared = 2 + 4 - .8 = 5.2 neighborhoods cleared by Friday

- If there are 10 total neighborhoods, and 5.2 were cleared, that is approximately 50% of neighborhoods that were cleared)

125. c (5 tons per day x 5 days , 5 x 5 = 25 tons)

Chapter 7: Visualization

126. Find these 2 patterns in the graphic image below:

127. If the pattern continues, what would be the 16th object?

    a. ∞
    b. ∞∞
    c. ∅
    d. ✻

128. How many times can you find the pattern in the graphic image below?

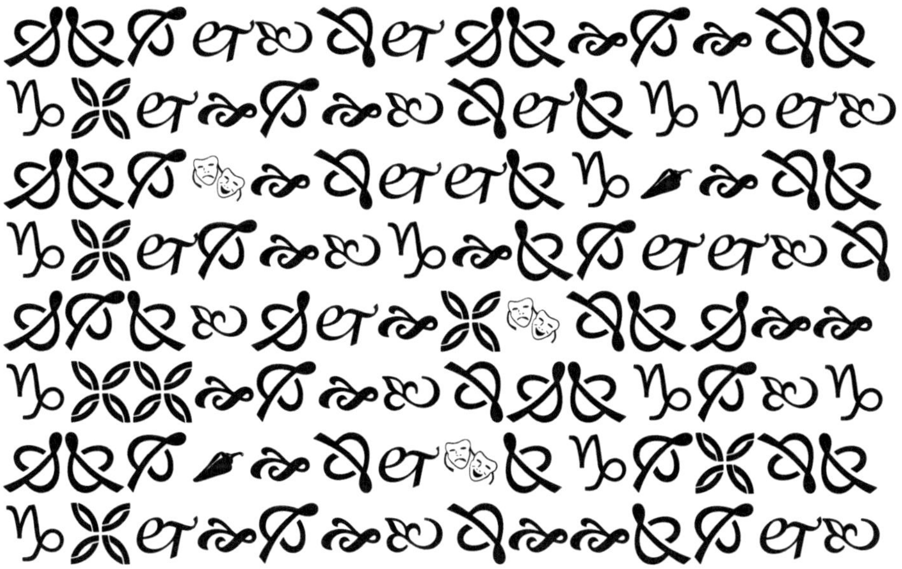

a. 4
b. 3
c. 2
d. 1

129. How many times can you find the number 896?

896   733   698   373   373   121   698
373   121   698   121   698   896   373   733   111
896   733   698   373   121   698   121
698   896   373   733   111   896   698   896   111
121   111   733   111   111   111   896   337
111   111   896   698   896   337   986   773
869   337   373   111   68   986   111

a. 11
b. 2
c. 9
d. 4

130. How many times do you see the number 741?

471   741417   174   414   414   104   174
414   104   174   104   174   471   414   741417
471   741417   174   414   104
174   104   174   471   414   741417   1011   471   174
471   104   1011   741417   1011   1011   1011
471
1011   1011   471   174   471   741   1114
104411   741   414   1011   414   1114   1011
104   1011   741417   1011   1011   1011   471

a. 10
b. 2
c. 3
d. 8

SANITATION WORKER EXAM PREP BOOK

131. Which group of shapes below, when assembled will form the large triangle below?

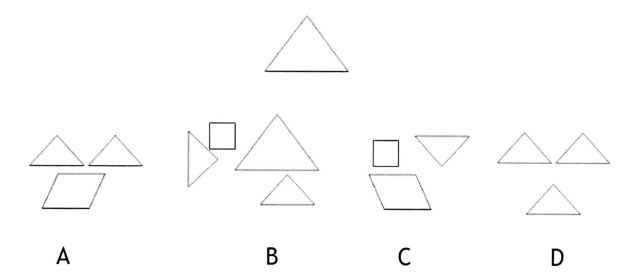

132. Which 2 objects when combined will form the one below?

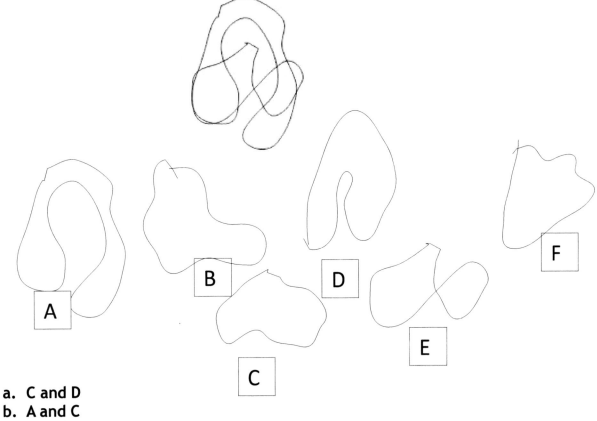

a. C and D
b. A and C
c. D and E
d. A and E

133. Based on the set of shapes below, which statement is correct?

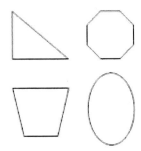

a. The octagon is to the top of the ellipse.
b. The trapezoid is to the top of the triangle.
c. The octagon is above the ellipse.

134. When unfolded, the box below look like which one of the possible selections?

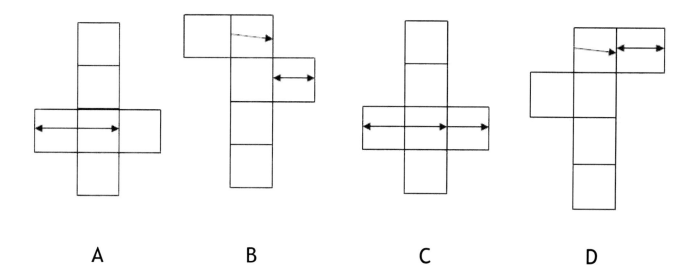

A   B   C   D

Chapter 7: VISUALIZATION

Answers for questions 126-134

126.

127. a

128. b

129. c

130. d

131. a

132. d

133. c

134. d

Chapter 9: LAWS & REGULATIONS

THE NEW YORK CITY RECYCLING LAW

Summary: The New York City Recycling Law, originally enacted in 1989 as Local Law 19, established the overarching "policy of the city to promote the recovery of materials from the New York City solid waste stream for the purpose of recycling such materials and returning them to the economy". This Law mandates recycling in NYC by residents, agencies, institutions, and businesses, including the designation of what materials are to be considered recyclable, the recovery of those materials, tonnages of recyclable materials that must be recycled annually, and responsibilities of each relevant party. The Rules were developed by DSNY to detail the requirements, operations, implementation and enforcement of mandated recycling including residential, agency and institutional, commercial, yard waste, and street events.

Amendments:
Local Law 40 of 2010 establishes diversion rates through 2020 for department managed waste.

The NYC Recycling Law has been amended several times. For additional amendments, please see the appropriate section in the left hand navigation for specific amendments.

NYC SOLID WASTE MANAGEMENT PLAN (SWMP)

Summary: NYC is tasked by NY State Solid Waste Management Policy to develop and periodically update solid waste management plan (SWMP). The state approved the City's first SWMP in 1992. A 1996 SWMP Update and Modification focused on the expansion of recycling. A 2000 SWMP Modification defined the phased closure of Fresh Kills Landfill. The 2006 SWMP provides a framework for establishing an "effective, reliable, and environmentally sound system" for managing the City's waste over the next 20 years. This planning document addresses three primary areas: waste prevention and recycling, long term export, and commercial waste.

NYC YARD WASTE COMPOSTING LAW

Summary: The NYC Yard Waste Composting Law, enacted as Local Law 40 of 2006, amended the NYC Recycling Law to further define the legal yard waste curbside set-out requirements for NYC residents, and how yard waste generated by landscapers and city agencies (such as the NYC Dept of Parks and Recreation) is supposed to be handled and transported to permitted composting facilities. The law also details penalties for non-compliance and bans the disposal of yard waste during selected times of year.

The Rules developed by DSNY detail the collection, removal, and handling of yard waste from residential buildings.

Amendments: Local Law 50 of 2003 temporarily suspended yard waste collection by DSNY from July 1, 2003 to June 30, 2004. Local Law 37 of 2010 updates the Yard Waste Composting Law to require DSNY to provide leaf and yard waste collection at NYC Housing Authority residential buildings, and composting of leaf and yard waste source-separated by City Agencies. DSNY is required to compost the leaf and yard waste it collects at one or more composting facilities operated by DSNY or on behalf of DSNY with the goal of eventually siting at least one facility in every borough where leaf and yard waste is collected. The law also requires annual reporting from all permitted composting facilities in the city and bans the disposal of grass clippings by residents during designated yard waste collection periods.

NYC ORGANIC WASTE COLLECTION

Summary: Local Law 77 amends the NYC Recycling Law to include requirements for DSNY to test a collection system for organic waste for composting or recycling between October 1, 2013 and July 1, 2015. It is voluntary for residents in pilot areas and mandatory for selected schools to set-out organic material during the pilot program. Local Law 77 concurrently suspends residential leaf and yard waste collection across certain neighborhoods of the City that generate large amounts of yard waste (required by Section 16-308 of the NYC Administrative Code), until July 1, 2016.

NYC CHRISTMAS TREE COLLECTION LAW

Summary: The NYC Recycling Law outlines the requirements for DSNY to establish a collection system for Christmas trees for composting or recycling during January of each year. It is voluntary for residents to set-out Christmas trees during the designated collection times.

NY STATE COMPOSTING FACILITIES AND PROCESSING LAW

Summary: The NY State Environmental Conservation Law governs the siting and operation of solid waste management and resource recovery facilities in the state, including composting and other organic waste processing (OWP) facilities. The NYS Dept of Environmental Conservation regulates the construction and operation composting and OWP facilities through permitting, testing, record keeping, and reporting requirements for each facility, and mandatory processing standards to minimize contamination and odor generation, eliminate pathogens, and produce a mature product.

NYC ELECTRONICS EQUIPMENT COLLECTION, RECYCLING AND REUSE ACT

Summary: The Electronic Equipment Collection Recycling and Reuse Act, enacted as Local Law 13 of 2008, requires electronics manufacturers that sell products in NYC to accept their products for recycling at no cost to the consumer. Covered electronics are banned from disposal by any person or entity in NYC starting July 1, 2010. The Rules, developed by DSNY, define covered electronics, take-back requirements, and the responsibilities of relevant parties.

Amendments: Local Law 21 of 2008 amended the electronics law to require manufacturers to comply with specific electronic waste collection performance standards.

NY STATE ELECTRONIC EQUIPMENT RECYCLING AND REUSE ACT

Summary: The NY State Electronic Equipment Recycling and Reuse Act law enacted as Chapter 99 of the Laws of 2010, establishes annual statewide recycling or reuse goals for all electronics waste and requires manufacturers of covered electronic equipment to establish a convenient system for the collection, handling, and recycling or reuse of discarded electronic waste, starting in 2011.

The law also phases in a disposal ban for discarded electronics. Electronics disposal is banned by any manufacturer, retailer, or owner or operator of an electronic waste collection site, electronic waste consolidation facility or electronic waste recycling facility by April 1, 2011, any person other than an individual or household by January 1, 2012, and by any individual or household by **January 1, 2015.**

NYC RECHARGEABLE BATTERY LAW

Summary: The New York City Rechargeable Battery Law, enacted as Local Law 97 of 2005 bans the disposal of rechargeable batteries in the regular trash (or in residential recycling containers) in NYC, and requires all NYC stores (except small food stores) that sell rechargeable batteries or products containing rechargeable batteries to accept up to ten batteries of the same shape and size as they sell, requires manufacturers to pay for the cost of their collection and disposal.

NYC REFRIGERANT RECYCLING LAW

Summary: Local Law 69 of 2013 was enacted to establish a manufacturer funded program for the recovery of refrigerants from refrigerant-containing appliances that are being disposed of by residential generators in the City of New York effective July 1, 2014.

NYC TEXTILE COLLECTION BIN LAWS

Summary: Local Law 38 of 2010 amended the NYC Recycling Law to establish a citywide textile reuse and recycling program that provides for the recovery of textiles by placing department-approved publicly accessible textile drop-off bins at convenient drop-off locations for all city residents. The law defines labeling requirements for the bins and reporting requirements for textiles collected. Local Law 34 of 2010 defines penalties for impermissibly placed collection bins.

While the use of collection bins to accept items for donation is voluntary, Local Law 31 of 2007 establishes requirements for the siting of any outdoor container (other than those placed by a government entity) that enables the public to deposit items for donation, such as clothing.

NY STATE AUTO BATTERY REGULATIONS

Summary: A lead-acid battery recycling statute was established as part of the NY State Environmental Conservation Law to facilitate the collection and recycling of lead-acid batteries by prohibiting the improper disposal of lead-acid batteries, establishing a financial incentive for the return of used batteries, and requiring lead-acid battery retailers and distributors to accept used batteries free of charge from the public.

Lead acid battery management and facilities are generally subject to hazardous waste management or universal waste regulations with certain exceptions.

NY STATE MERCURY THERMOSTAT COLLECTION ACT

Summary: The Mercury Thermostat Collection Act requires manufacturers to establish and maintain a program for the collection, transportation, recycling, and proper management of out-of-service mercury thermostats at no cost to the consumer or other persons participating in the program. The purpose of the Act is to increase the convenience of safe drop-off and recycling of out-of-service mercury thermostats for consumers, thus diverting them from landfills. It is illegal to dispose of mercury thermostats in the trash. NY State has had a ban in place since 2005.

NY STATE MOTOR OIL REGULATIONS

Summary: The NY State Environmental Conservation Law directs the proper handling, recycling and disposal of used oil, which includes any oil or lubricant product refined from crude or synthetic oil, including motor oil. Used oil is prohibited from disposal by the public. Most service stations and certain retailers are required to accept used oil from the public. The NY State Dept of Environmental Conservation regulates generators, transporters, processors, refiners, energy recovery, and transfer facilities that handle used oil. NYSDEC also provides standards for the marketing of used oil as a fuel.

NY STATE SHARPS COLLECTION LAW

Summary: The NY State Public Health Law was amended, as part of Chapter 438 of the Laws of 1993 to require hospitals and nursing homes to accept sharps, including syringes and lancets from residents provided the materials are brought in a puncture proof container. The regulations define regulated medical waste and describe proper containment, storage, transfer, and disposal of sharps.

NY STATE WASTE TIRE MANAGEMENT AND RECYCLING ACT

Summary: The Waste Tire Management and Recycling Act of 2003 was enacted to ensure the proper management of waste tires in NY State. This Law established a waste tire management and recycling fee per new tire sold to be deposited in a Waste Tire Management and Recycling Fund, and required the NY State Dept of Environmental Conservation (NYSDEC) to prepare a comprehensive plan to abate all noncompliant waste tire stockpiles in the state. Landfilling of waste tires is prohibited unless NYSDEC determines that it is not feasible to convert the waste tires to a beneficial use. Tire service centers must accept from customers used tires of an equivalent size and quantity of new tires purchased or installed.

NYSDEC also regulates waste tire storage facilities and waste tire processing facilities.

NY STATE WIRELESS RECYCLING ACT

Summary: The New York State Wireless Recycling Act, enacted as Chapter 730 of the Laws of 2006 requires all wireless telephone service providers that sell cell phones in the State of New York to accept up to 10 cell phones from any person for reuse or recycling or provide a method for shipping the phones for recycling at no cost, effective January 1, 2007.

NYC ASBESTOS ABATEMENT LAW

Summary: NYC's asbestos abatement law, originally established by Local Law 76 of 1985, mandates removal of asbestos from buildings facing renovation or demolition, and that workers handling asbestos receive appropriate training. The Rules of the NYC Asbestos Control Program are under the authority of the NYC Dept of Environmental Protection in consultation with the NYC Dept of Buildings and the NYC Fire Dept.

Amendments: Local Law 37 of 2009 adds asbestos abatement project permitting requirements and specifications for temporary structures for abatement activities. Local Law 38 of 2009 requires updates to the rules regarding egress at abatement sites.

NYC ASBESTOS TRANSPORT, STORAGE, AND DISPOSAL LAW

Summary: The transportation, storage, and disposal of asbestos or asbestos contaminated materials are regulated by the NYC Dept of Sanitation. Local Law 70 of 1985 and related rules establish requirements for the proper transport, storage, and disposal of asbestos waste after these materials have been removed from a construction site.

NY STATE FLUORESCENT LAMP MANAGEMENT REGULATIONS

Summary: The Mercury-Added Consumer Products Law mandates that waste products containing mercury, including fluorescent lamps, must be properly labeled and managed separately from solid waste. Households are exempt and may discard fluorescent bulbs in the trash. Businesses, however, must handle all mercury-containing bulbs (including low-mercury or non-hazardous "green end cap" lamps) according to either hazardous waste or universal waste standards. Small businesses less than 100 employees that discard 15 or fewer low-mercury (non-hazardous "green end cap") bulbs per month are also exempt.

Chapter 10: GLOSSARY OF HELPFUL TERMS TO KNOW

ACRONYMS	
BWPRR	Bureau of Waste Prevention, Reuse and Recycling
C & D	Construction and demolition debris
CDs	Community Districts
CENYC	Council on the Environment of New York City
CEQR	City Environmental Quality Review
CNG	Compressed natural gas
DSNY	New York City Department of Sanitation
EBUF	Enclosed barge unloading facility
FWD	Food waste disposals
FY	Fiscal Year
HHW	Household Hazardous Waste
LL 19	Local Law 19 of 1989
LL 74	Local Law 74 of 2000
LL 87	Local Law 87 of 1992
MGP	Metal, glass and plastic
MRF	Material recovery facility
MSW	Municipal solid waste
MTS	Marine transfer station
N/A	Not Applicable

NYCDEP	New York City Department of Environmental Conservation
NYCDOT	New York City Department of Transportation
NYCDPR	New York City Department of Parks and Recreation
NYCEDC	New York City Economic Development Corporation
NYCRR	New York Codes, Rules and Regulations
NYMTC	New York Metropolitan Transportation Council
NYSDEC	New York State Department of Environmental Conservation
PIU	Permit and Inspection Unit
RCNY	Rules of the City of New York
RDF	Refuse derived fuel
RRF	Resource Recovery Facility
SBMT	South Brooklyn Marine Terminal
SWMP	Final Comprehensive Solid Waste Management Plan, September 2006
TPD	Tons per day
TPY	Tons per year
TS	Transfer Station
ULSD	Ultra-low-sulfur diesel
USEPA	United States Environmental Protection Agency
WCS	Waste Characterization Study

DEFINITIONS	
1992 SWMP	The City's first Comprehensive Solid Waste Management Plan, approved by NYS DEC in 1992
1996 SWMP	The update and modification to the 1992SWMP, approved by NYSDEC in 1996
2000 SWMP	The modification to the 1992 SWMP, adopted by the City Council in 2000 and approved by NYSDEC in 2001
Administrative Code	Administrative Code of the City of New York
Alternative(s)	An alternative to the Proposed Action evaluated in the SWMP DEIS
Bureau of Cleaning and Collections	The DSNY Bureau that collects the residential and institutional components of DSNY-managed Waste, and cleans and removes snow from City streets
Bureau of Planning and Budget's Operations Management Division	The Bureau that provides budget and planning oversight of DSNY operations
Bureau of Waste Disposal	The Bureau that manages waste export
C&D debris	Waste from construction-related activity that is defined as Non-Putrescible Waste in the DSNY Rules
City	New York City
City Council	The legislative body of the City of New York
Commercial Waste	The wastes, including recycled material, generated in the City by business establishments and construction activity and collected by private carters that are respectively defined in the DSNY Rules as Putrescible Waste and Non-Putrescible Waste
Containerized Waste	Waste loaded into intermodal containers that can be carried on rail cars or barges

Converted MTS	One of the marine transfer stations that are elements of the Proposed Action and which would be modified to containerize waste for out-of-City export by barge or rail
Curbside Recycling Program or Curbside Program	The collection of source-separated paper and metal, glass and plastic (MGP) designated by DSNY as Recyclables from residences, City agencies and non-profit institutions housed in tax-exempt property
Curbside MGP Program	The collection of metal, glass and plastic Recyclables through the Curbside Program
Curbside Recyclables	Paper and MGP collected through the Curbside Program
CWM Study	The Commercial Waste Management Study mandated by LL 74 and issued by DSNY in March 2004
DSNY-managed Waste	Solid waste that DSNY collects from all residential households in the City, waste collected by other DSNY operations, such as lot cleaning and self-help drop-off, and the institutional waste of City, state and federal agencies and non-profit institutions that DSNY collects and/or for which DSNY arranges disposal
Essex County RRF	Essex County Resource Recovery Facility in Newark, New Jersey
Fill Material	A category of Non-Putrescible Waste defined in the DSNY Rules that is processed and stored at Fill Material Transfer Stations in the City
Fill Material Transfer Station	A facility permitted by DSNY to process Fill Material
Food Center	Hunts Point Food Distribution Center
Golden Apple Awards Program	Encourages waste prevention, recycling and neighborhood cleanup efforts in City schools through cash awards and the recognition of achievements

Interim Export	Short-term DSNY contracts with in- and out-of-City transfer stations and out-of-City disposal sites for export of DSNY-managed Waste
Long Term Export Program	Those SWMP facilities and services that will, to the extent practicable, provide for the containerization of DSNY-managed Waste and its export from the City by barge or rail
Marine Transfer Station (MTS) Conversion Program	The design, permitting and construction activities to develop, at existing MTS sites, facilities to containerize waste for long-term export
Milestones	A schedule of activities to implement the Proposed Actions and New Initiatives
MTS RFP, MTS Containerization RFP	DSNY's Request for Proposals to Transport and Dispose of Containerized Waste from One or More Marine Transfer Stations, issued December 22, 2003
New Initiatives	New activities described in the SWMP that are enhancements to Existing Programs
Non-Putrescible Commercial Waste	Inert waste generated from commercial and residential demolition, new construction and renovation projects, comprised of inorganic materials, some of which are recycled. The non-recycled fraction is processed by the City's Non-Putrescible Transfer Stations for shipment to disposal facilities. This waste is also referred to as construction and demolition (C&D) debris to distinguish it from Fill Material, which is a subset of Non- Putrescible Waste comprised of materials such as excavated fill, stone rubble and road millings that are graded into materials such as sand and aggregate and stockpiled at Fill Material Transfer Stations in the City and reused in other building projects
Non-Putrescible Waste Transfer Station	A facility permitted by DSNY to process Non-Putrescible Waste

Putrescible Commercial Waste	Material generated by business establishments and collected by private carters in the City that may be delivered to putrescible transfer stations or recycled, which may contain organic matter
Putrescible Waste Transfer Station	A facility permitted by DSNY to process Putrescible Waste
Recyclables	Materials defined by DSNY as recyclable such as Paper and MGP
Rules	Rules of the City of New York
Special Waste	Materials that are a subset of Household Hazardous Waste
Preliminary Waste Characterization	First recyclables and refuse waste characterization since 1989/90 study, based on sorts conducted in May and June of 2004
SWMP	The Final Comprehensive Solid Waste Management Plan for the period 2006 through 2025 prepared pursuant to 6 NYCRR Part 360-15
Waste Prevention and Recycling Program	Activities undertaken by DSNY to cause or promote the prevention, reuse, recycling or composting of waste

RESOURCES SECTION
Provided to you by www.nyccivilserviceexams.com

As promised in our Ebook, with this document we are providing you with some internet links/resources for you to further study/practice for the Sanitation Worker Exam.

All these resources/websites are free. You do not need to pay for anything. If there are any ads on the sites, don't pay/buy for anything. There is plenty of free information on the internet, you just need to know where to look to find it. We do not receive any commission for any of the resources included in this list. We would simply like to see you follow our Recipe for Passing and study further to increase your chances of passing the Sanitation Worker Exam in February 2015.

After you've read our book and identified which areas you could use more help with, you should focus on that specific area. When visiting these links, use the key words for the area you need help with (we listed them again at the end of the 2nd page for your reference and they are in your book as well).

One more thing we would like to share with you is something called 'Open Courseware'. In case you aren't aware of what this is: basically it's College and High School courses for free online. Since they are free you do not receive College Credit or a College Degree, but you gain knowledge at the comfort and convenience of your own home and schedule. There is a worldwide movement where Colleges and Universities are offering classes for free online for various subjects. We have listed some of those here for you as well. You can target the specific areas you need more help with for the Sanitation Exam, or you can just learn something new and expand your knowledge.

Best website for help with Math: www.khanacademy.org

https://www.khanacademy.org/math/pre-algebra

https://www.youtube.com/watch?v=Q5gk9ljVuTE

http://ocw.usu.edu/English/introduction-to-writing-academic-prose/inductive-and-deductive-reasoning.html

http://www.brown.edu/Departments/Philosophy/onlinepapers/schechter/DeductiveReasoning.pdf

http://changingminds.org/disciplines/argument/types_reasoning/deduction.htm

http://quizlet.com/15564826/deductiveinductive-reasoning-flash-cards/

University of Oxford on ITUNES has a lot of courses (you do not need and Iphone or Ipad, all you need is have/download Itunes on your computer):

https://itunes.apple.com/us/itunes-u/critical-reasoning-for-beginners/id387875756?mt=10

http://www.aarp.org/health/brain-health/brain_games/

http://vimeo.com/81284403

http://www.slideshare.net/karunsthakur/prepare-for-aptitude-test?related=1

http://collegeopentextbooks.org/opentextbookcontent/open-textbooks-by-subject/englishandcomposition

OPEN COURSEWARE-FREE ONLINE CLASSES GIVEN BY COLLEGES & UNIVERSITIES:

https://en.wikipedia.org/wiki/EdX

https://www.edx.org/course-search

http://www.oeconsortium.org/courses/category/

For example, this course is an Introduction to Algebra:

https://www.edx.org/course/schoolyourself/schoolyourself-algebrax-introduction-3731#.VG1ABfnF_T8

Areas of focus for the Sanitation Worker Exam
Written and Reading Comprehension
Problem Sensitivity
Written Expression
Information Ordering
Deductive Reasoning
Spatial Orientation
Mathematics
Visualization

We've vetted all websites included in this list as of November 2014. If any of the links are broken or if you should receive website errors, we apologize as we have no control over this (these are not our websites). Feel free to email us and let us know and we will update our list.

BEST OF LUCK ON THE EXAM!

 There is no such thing as can't.
-Christopher Reeve

Are you thinking about taking more Civil Service Exams? Then please visit our website for more Exam Prep Books Coming Soon as well as even more resources to help you in your studying...

****When you by more than 1 book, you will get a Customer Loyalty discount****

www.nyccivilserviceexams.com